DENNIS BRUTUS

**Discover history's heroes
and their stories.**

Michael Collins

Susan La Flesche Picotte

Ida B. Wells

DISCOVERING HISTORY'S HEROES

HEROES

DENNIS BRUTUS

BY CRAIG ELLENPORT

Aladdin

New York London Toronto Sydney New Delhi

ALADDIN

An imprint of Simon & Schuster Children's Publishing Division

1230 Avenue of the Americas, New York, New York 10020

First Aladdin hardcover edition May 2021

Text copyright © 2021 by Craig Ellenport

Jacket illustration copyright © 2021 by Lisa K. Weber

Also available in an Aladdin paperback edition.

For information about special discounts for bulk purchases,
please contact Simon & Schuster Special Sales
at 1-866-506-1949 or business@simonandschuster.com.

The Simon & Schuster Speakers Bureau can bring authors to your live
event. For more information or to book an event contact the
Simon & Schuster Speakers Bureau at 1-866-248-3049
or visit our website at www.simonspeakers.com.

Jacket designed by Heather Palisi

Interior designed by Mike Rosamilia

The text of this book was set in Adobe Caslon Pro.

Manufactured in the United States of America 0321 FFG

2 4 6 8 10 9 7 5 3 1

Library of Congress Control Number 2020949301

ISBN 978-1-5344-6236-6 (hc)

ISBN 978-1-5344-6235-9 (pbk)

ISBN 978-1-5344-6237-3 (eBook)

CONTENTS

DENNIS BRUTUS

1.
PROFESSOR BRUTUS

It was a warm, sunny day on the campus at Northwestern University in Evanston, Illinois. Professor Dennis Brutus was walking to his afternoon African Literature class in University Hall, on the south side of campus. The significance of the nice weather was not lost on Professor Brutus. He knew that the lecture he had prepared for his students was not going to be given—at least not this day.

Brutus wanted to talk to his students about award-winning South African author Nadine Gordimer, but his students had other plans. It wasn't that they weren't interested in Gordimer or what Professor Brutus had to say about her work. They had other things on their minds. Five minutes from University Hall, in the area where Northwestern's administrative buildings were located, the school's Anti-Apartheid Alliance had been conducting a sit-in for several days.

The year was 1985, and school **protests** like these were commonplace around the United States. College students in the United States of America were vocal in their objection to **apartheid**—the system of **segregation** that oppressed the black population in the country of South Africa. Even though the majority of the population of South Africa was made up of blacks and people of mixed race, it was the white minority that controlled the government. Apartheid had been put in place so that things would remain that way.

Racial segregation had been taking place in South Africa for decades, but it became worse in 1948. That was when the National Party came into power. They made racial segregation an official government policy. And they gave it an official name: apartheid. Over the years, different groups had tried to put pressure on the white leaders in South Africa to end apartheid, but up until 1985, nothing had changed the policy.

The anti-apartheid movement on college campuses in the United States in the late eighties grew fast and gained much attention. Young people in the United States came to learn about the symbol of the movement, Nelson Mandela, a black man who had been imprisoned in South Africa since 1963.

Professor Brutus knew all about Mandela. For a year and a half, Dennis Brutus had occupied the jail cell next to Mandela.

Professor Brutus entered his classroom, and the requests were immediate:

"Professor Brutus, it's such a nice day. Can we have class outside?"

They all knew what that meant. "Outside" meant

walking over to the area where the Anti-Apartheid Alliance was holding its sit-in. And as soon as they got there, the Alliance would ask Professor Brutus to speak. But they didn't want him to speak about African Literature.

The professor suggested maybe they should just have the class in the classroom, but he knew his students were determined to go outside and take part in what the Anti-Apartheid Alliance was doing. Professor Brutus knew his lecture would be out the window. But that was okay.

Literature was important to Brutus, who had written several books of poetry that were considered to be very good. But he also appreciated that his young students recognized the importance of protest. Protest, after all, was what had gotten Brutus thrown into jail in the first place.

Protest was what had gotten him tortured and shot.

Protest was why he'd been forced to leave the

country he'd grown up in, and had not been allowed to return for many years.

I know all about this scene because I was there. It was my junior year at Northwestern, and I was a student in Professor Brutus's African Literature class. I had also been involved with the Anti-Apartheid Alliance, so when Brutus did agree to move our class outside and speak to the gathered students, it was very special.

It was also awe-inspiring. Dennis Brutus was more than just one of the most acclaimed poets in the history of South Africa. Here, in front of us, was a man who had taken a stand against what he knew was wrong. He had known that he was risking his life in the process, but he never backed away from the cause. And his actions made a difference.

After that spring semester, I went back home to New York. An aspiring journalist, I had a summer job with a popular sports magazine. I also kept in touch with Professor Brutus and spoke with him that summer. The professor took a surprising interest in my job.

At first it seemed odd that a poet and teacher from South Africa would take an interest in an American sports magazine. When you dig into Brutus's past, however, it makes sense.

Sports, after all, was the vehicle for Dennis Brutus's protest of apartheid in the 1960s. Brutus had helped lead a group that had pressured the International Olympic Committee to **ban** South Africa from participating in the Olympics until the country abolished apartheid. South Africa *was* eventually banned from the Olympics. What Brutus did in the 1960s might be one of the earliest examples of how sports can have an important influence on human culture. The Olympics ban didn't end apartheid, but it raised awareness around the world.

Through the years there have been many occasions when sporting events have provided an opportunity for protesting social or political issues of the day. Ironically, Brutus had originally intended his protest to be just about sports, specifically the apartheid policies that were unfair to South African athletes. But the more involved he got—and the more he was viewed as a thorn in the side of South Africa's apartheid government—the more Brutus became a symbol of the overall movement to abolish apartheid.

"Mr. Brutus has a distinction that makes him a hated symbol to the white rulers of South Africa, and a heroic one to the critics of their regime," Anthony Lewis wrote in the *New York Times* in 1983. "He has actually succeeded in bringing about some change in one aspect of apartheid."[1]

The anti-apartheid protests that were taking place at Northwestern and other college campuses across the United States did more than just build awareness of the problem. The protests were designed to convince colleges and universities to **divest** from South Africa. Students wanted their schools to stop investing money in companies that operated in South

Africa. In other words, students wanted to fight apartheid financially. If South African businesses started losing money because of apartheid, that would be another way the government would feel pressure to change its policies. Slowly but surely, the government did change.

By the 1990s, South Africa finally abandoned its apartheid policies. The country changed dramatically.

Dennis Brutus—poet, teacher, activist, and one of the key voices that helped end apartheid in South Africa.

This is his story.

2.
GROWING UP

Dennis Brutus was born on November 28, 1924, in
Salisbury, a town in the British **colony** of Southern Rhodesia. Today that area is part of the country
of Zimbabwe, which is just north of South Africa.
When Dennis was four, his family moved south to
Port Elizabeth, a seaport located in the southeastern
part of South Africa, on the Indian Ocean.

Dennis was the third of four children in his
family. Wilfred, his brother, was four years older;
his sister Helen was two years older than Dennis;

and his sister Dolly was two years younger.

Dennis's mother and father were both children of mixed marriages—they each had one parent who was white and one who was black. Because of this, the family was classified as "colored" when they moved to Port Elizabeth. In South Africa, even before apartheid was an official government policy, there was a strong class distinction among whites, blacks, and coloreds. Whites had an advantage over both blacks and coloreds.

Dennis's parents were teachers. Later in his life Dennis recalled that his mother was very friendly and very popular. He remembered his father as being very serious and quiet. On most weekdays his father left the house early in the morning and did not come home until the kids were asleep at night. That was because, on top of teaching, he worked part-time jobs at night to help support the family.

One of Mr. Brutus's jobs was as an accountant for a friend who owned a fruit shop. In addition to getting paid, Dennis's father also got to bring home fresh fruit. Dennis remembered a game his father would play on weekends. He would bring a wrapped package of fruit into the room and invite the kids to guess what kind of fruit it was by smelling it. Sometimes it was apples. Sometimes it was oranges or bananas. Whatever kind of fruit it was, Mr. Brutus would then cut it into four pieces for the children to share.

It wasn't until Dennis was older that he came to understand that his father was "a man of considerable brilliance."[2] Mr. Brutus had helped create the Teachers' League of South Africa, an important organization for colored teachers. The goal of the Teachers' League was to bring black and colored teachers together to improve the quality of their schools.

Dennis recalled that his father was often tough on him, partly because his mother may have been overprotective. "I think I was regarded as delicate," he wrote in his **autobiography**, noting that he often got nosebleeds as a child, sometimes the result of fighting with his older brother.[3] The nosebleeds would cause his mother to be worried and anxious. This irritated his father.

His father also got annoyed sometimes when he thought Dennis wasn't paying attention. His mother, on the other hand, looked at it differently. She called him "Freddie Far-Off." That was the name of a character in a children's book who used to daydream about magical adventures. She said Dennis was just daydreaming.

Dennis thought his father might have played favorites with his children, caring more for Wilfred and Helen. But he thought his father treated them equally when it came to sharing his love of reading. About once a month, Mr. Brutus would let them go through his encyclopedia. He would share his books about British history and the Roman empire.

Wilfred went to one of the better **missionary** schools for nonwhite children, and the school had a library of mostly used books that had been passed on from white schools. Wilfred would bring home a book once a week, and Dennis always enjoyed reading these. He particularly enjoyed books about King Arthur and other medieval legends.

Dennis's father also shared with his children his love of poetry. Dennis remembered listening to his father recite poetry—often while shaving. Mr. Brutus was a big fan of the work of Alfred, Lord Tennyson. One poem Dennis remembered hearing often was Tennyson's "Ode on the Death of the Duke of Wellington."

Sometimes his father would ask Dennis and his siblings to recite poetry for him. And his father would then teach them how to improve their delivery—how to better articulate what they were reading, with emphasis on different words or with a pause in just the right place. When Dennis later recited his own poetry as a grown man, he would use the tips he'd learned from his father.

Between their father's love of reading and their mother's love of music, the Brutus children grew up in a smart, cultured environment. But they still had their share of problems to deal with.

When Dennis was eleven, he went to a Catholic school called St. Theresa's, which was run by Catholic nuns. St. Theresa's was located in a white area, so just walking to school presented problems. The white kids would throw stones and bottles at the blacks and coloreds, who would in turn defend themselves and fight back. It wasn't unusual for the police to be called.

"When the police arrived," Dennis explained, "invariably they would take the side of the white kids, even if we were in the right and had been assaulted by much bigger kids."[4]

Money was also an issue for Dennis's family. There were not many opportunities for coloreds to advance and succeed in South Africa. His parents could not get jobs at the better schools, because those schools were only for whites, and blacks and colored people were not allowed to work there.

Even with his father working extra jobs at night, the family struggled to make ends meet. This slowly but surely became a strain on his parents' marriage.

When Dennis was about twelve years old, his mother took a teaching job at a school in Grahamstown, which was about a hundred miles away from Port Elizabeth. She moved there temporarily. At first she took her two daughters, Helen and Dolly, with her. After a few months, she came back for Dennis and Wilfred.

They returned to Port Elizabeth a year or two later, but Dennis's father would not take them back. Dennis, his mother, and his siblings stayed with friends who lived on Charlotte Street. It was not a good situation. Dennis recalled sleeping on the floor and washing dishes or running errands when he wasn't in school.

During that time, Dennis's father served his mother with divorce papers. Dennis remembered how traumatic it was for her to deal with her lawyers.

They were taking a long time to settle the divorce, which meant they could charge his mother more money. Dennis helped her draft letters for the lawyers. But when he saw how upset his mother was over the situation, he decided to go one step further and put his powers of persuasion to work. He met with the lawyers to tell them to stop making demands on his mother. He argued that they were treating her unfairly.

Dennis was fifteen years old at this time. He didn't think the lawyers would pay that much attention to a teenager, but they did. They left his mother alone. This might have been the first time that Dennis had had the experience of seeing his words make a significant impact.

In many ways, Dennis's childhood set him up for the life that was ahead of him. Being the child of two teachers, he could imagine becoming a teacher himself. Reading and learning about poetry at a young age would inspire him to write his own poetry. Growing up in poverty taught him the need to work hard in order to overcome obstacles.

Dennis's experience with his mother's divorce lawyers was another building block for the future. It gave him the confidence to speak up in protest if he saw something he thought was wrong.

3.
EARLY POETRY, TEACHING, AND SPORTS

When Dennis was a young child, he liked playing school. He enjoyed telling other kids the stories from the books his father had given him about Roman history. But Dennis didn't love going to school. He thought some of the teachers at St. Theresa's were very mean. They were more interested in making sure students were quiet than they were interested in teaching them. It wasn't until Dennis moved on to Paterson High School in Port Elizabeth that he started taking a greater interest in his schooling.

In addition to his classwork, Dennis also participated in sports at Paterson. He played soccer and cricket. Dennis would have been the first to tell you that he wasn't a very good athlete, but he still enjoyed playing. Soccer, cricket, and rugby are all team sports, and he liked the idea of teamwork.

Dennis liked playing sports, but he also liked watching sports. His father had encouraged him as a boy to keep a scrapbook of pictures and stories of great athletes. Athletes like Milo Pillay.

Around the time that Dennis's mother had first gone to Grahamstown, the 1936 Summer Olympics were being held in Berlin. Milo Pillay was a South African–born Indian who ran a club for weight lifters. At the South African Olympic Games trials, Pillay had been the only weight lifter chosen out of seventeen competitors to represent South Africa at the Berlin Olympic Games.

But the government would not allow Pillay to go. Because he was colored, his spot was given to a white man instead. It didn't matter that Pillay was better qualified. Under the country's policy, whites were treated better than people of color. Whites went to better schools, worked better jobs, and lived in better neighborhoods. And because he was colored, Milo Pillay was not allowed to represent his country in the Olympics.

The policy of treating whites better than people of color served to create racial inequality in South Africa. It did not have an official name at the time, but it came to be known as "apartheid."

It was still not known as "apartheid" when Dennis was going to Paterson High School. Some of the teachers at Paterson thought it was important to teach Dennis and his classmates about things the government was doing to create racial inequality. Dennis understood some of what was happening in politics, but he was more focused on high school life.

In addition to his sports activities, Dennis began to write poetry. His interest in poetry had first begun when he'd listened to his father reciting poetry while shaving and his mother reciting nursery rhymes.

But one of Dennis's first experiences *writing* poetry was the result of sibling rivalry.

He recalled writing his first poem at the age of fourteen or fifteen. It's nowhere to be found, but he said he wrote it about a full moon in August. He was fond of what he had written but wasn't motivated to write more poetry until his brother, Wilfred, came home from college during a holiday break.

"I discovered that he had acquired a mastery of Afrikaans," said Dennis in his autobiography.[5] In the area where he lived, Afrikaans and English were the two most common languages. Afrikaans had developed from the language of the early Dutch settlers who'd first come to South Africa in the 1800s. Most people in Port Elizabeth grew up speaking English, but Afrikaans was taught in school.

"This annoyed me very greatly," Dennis said of his brother's accomplishment, "because I hated to be outdone by him in anything. And when I learned that he had written some Afrikaans poetry for the school magazine, I felt I ought to write as well."[6]

Dennis began to write both English and Afrikaans poetry—mainly love poems. He found it was a good way for him to express his feelings for girls he liked. In high school he became friends with some other kids who liked to write poetry. He recalled that it was an excellent science teacher who encouraged them to start a student magazine. Dennis became the editor. Often, however, he was stuck with no articles to put into the publication. So he would sit down and write poems to fill the pages.

When he was in high school, Dennis's favorite poet was Robert Browning, a British poet from the 1800s. Browning was known for long, dramatic poetry. He often used a lot of big words.

Dennis was flattered when a teacher asked him to read a Browning passage in class. This might be too difficult for some, but Dennis enjoyed it. He remembered when he'd been younger and his father had taught him how to articulate what he was reading. Dennis was good at this, and he became known in school as an expert on Robert Browning.

For most nonwhites in South Africa at the time, high school was the end of their education. But Dennis liked school, and he wanted to go on to college. He was one of just fourteen nonwhite students in the area where he lived who took the college entrance exam. Of those fourteen, only four passed. Dennis was one of them.

The question now was how to pay for college. Dennis was afraid he couldn't afford to go. To his surprise, he was awarded a scholarship from the Port Elizabeth city council. He received enough money to pay for three years of college.

In 1944, Dennis arrived at the University of Fort Hare, on the Eastern Cape of South Africa. This university was one of the few colleges in South Africa for blacks.

Dennis was more than halfway through college when he realized he didn't have enough money to continue going to school full-time. Fortunately, he was able to take a year off from school and earn some money by teaching. He worked in a small village called Fort Beaufort, which was about fifteen miles west of Fort Hare. There he taught English, Afrikaans, history, and geography at the St. Michael's Catholic Mission, which was a junior high school. He lived in a small house that was attached to a church and spent nearly all his free time during that year writing poetry.

In his autobiography, Dennis said he wrote a hundred poems while he was in Fort Beaufort. He kept them in a notebook that he titled "Green Harvest." The word "green" can describe something that is youthful or inexperienced. Dennis knew these poems were not meant to be published. They were for himself.

One year later, he was back at Fort Hare, where he

was on the editorial staff of a student publication. He had at least one poem published, but he mostly wrote reviews of films and books.

Dennis graduated from Fort Hare in 1947. His two major subjects were psychology and English. Because of his experience teaching in Fort Beaufort, he also earned a teaching diploma.

Dennis returned to Port Elizabeth. He couldn't get a teaching job because the schools were all closed for vacation. His brother, Wilfred, was working as a porter on a train, moving equipment and sweeping the cars. The traveling sounded very glamorous to Dennis. He thought it would be a nice way to visit new places.

"It was much less glamorous than I expected," Dennis wrote in his autobiography.[7] He worked very hard while the train was going from one place to the next. So when they arrived in a new city, he was too exhausted to explore. The next morning, the train would be off and Dennis would be back to work.

When schools reopened after vacation, Dennis was asked to come teach classes at his old high school, Paterson. Brutus taught English, Afrikaans, and some Latin. After a short time at Paterson, he went to teach at St. Thomas Aquinas, a Catholic high school in Port Elizabeth. Dennis's parents were both Catholic, but he didn't teach religion at St. Thomas Aquinas.

In addition to teaching some classes at the high school, Dennis became the manager of the sports teams. He had continued to play soccer, cricket, and rugby throughout his college years, and he still enjoyed being around sports. He coached the softball and baseball teams. In one of the years when he served as coach, the softball team won the provincial trophy. In addition to coaching, he was also responsible for scheduling games and matches with other schools in all sports. Eventually he came to represent the school sports program in the local sports union. And after being promoted several times, he found himself chairman and delegate to the national body for school sports.

Over time, Dennis served as a delegate to more than half a dozen national sports organizations in different sports, including lawn tennis, table tennis, cricket, weight lifting, judo, boxing, softball, and baseball.

Dennis enjoyed working with sports. He didn't realize at the time that his experiences were preparing him for his future **activism**. He was gaining valuable contacts in the various governing bodies of sports, and he was learning the ins and outs of how to change policies and vote on new rules within these governing bodies.

"Without my being aware of it," he would later say, "I was being equipped with certain skills which really qualified me for a key job."[8]

Even in the years before apartheid officially became the policy in South Africa, Dennis experienced situations that made him keenly aware of the racial **discrimination** that was taking place throughout the country.

At other times Dennis was unaware of racial injustice. For example, he had befriended an Irish priest who had been very nice to him when Dennis was in high school. Dennis went to visit the priest in his home one day, and when he got to the house, he knocked on the front door. In those days, in South Africa, blacks did not go to the front door of a priest's house.

The priest wasn't mad about this, but when he came out, he said, "You know, I sometimes think that you forget you're black."[9]

When Dennis recalled this story in his autobiography, he laughed because what the priest had said was true.

"For me I was just a human being," he said. "I didn't feel that I was the inferior, and I interacted with people as equals whether they were white or black. But I remember this now as a kind of curious thing, and again I think it may have had something to do with this kind of absent-minded way I floated through the world."[10]

4.
STARTING A FAMILY, FIGHTING APARTHEID

May Jaggers grew up in Port Elizabeth and was a good friend of Dennis's younger sister, Dolly. May's mother passed away when she was very young, and then her father died in 1944, when May was fifteen years old. Suddenly an orphan, May spent a lot of time with the Brutus family. Dennis's mother cared for May as if she were part of their family.

Dennis liked May. He would see her whenever he came home from college during holidays. But they didn't spend a lot of time together. May and Dolly liked to go out with friends, to the movies, or to a party. Dennis preferred to stay home and read.

After college, when he came back to Port Elizabeth to teach, Dennis started spending more time with May. Eventually they became more than just friends.

In 1950, May Jaggers and Dennis Brutus were married.

Just as Dennis was starting to become more aware of the **racism** and inequality that was spreading throughout South Africa, so was May. She was never afraid to speak her mind about injustice. That was certainly one of the things that Dennis liked about her.

May was also a very caring person. Having grown up without a mother for most of her life, she got many of her motherly instincts from Dennis's mom. It wasn't long before May and Dennis had a family of their own.

Less than a year after they were married, Dennis and May welcomed their first child, Jacinta. She soon had a baby brother, Marc. Then came Julian. In 1955, Dennis and May had their fourth child, Tony.

They lived in a small house on Shell Street in Port Elizabeth. It would have been a crowded house with just two parents and the four children. But May had a lot of love to give, and she was happy to grow the family. After Tony came Tina. Then Cordelia, Greg, and Paula. Eight children!

May was a very caring and nurturing mother to her children. She was always there for them. Dennis, unfortunately, was not always there. As the family grew throughout the decade of the 1950s, so did Dennis's involvement in community activism.

The seeds of Dennis's activism had started to take root a few years before he and May had gotten married.

Whites had always been the minority in South Africa, but they controlled the government, and they created policies that would keep them in power. The Natives Land Act of 1913 made it so blacks and coloreds couldn't buy land in most areas of the country. Not only did the white minority control 80 percent of the land, but this act also made it so that blacks in South Africa were so spread out that it would be hard for them to come together to create any kind of organization strong enough to challenge the white authority.

In 1948, the same year Dennis began his teaching career, the National Party—made up mostly of the Dutch-descended, white Afrikaners—won the general election in South Africa. The National Party introduced the word "apartheid" as its campaign slogan. "Apartheid" means "apartness" in Afrikaans, and the goal of the National Party was to reinforce the policies that kept whites in power.

Within two years, apartheid gripped the country. To further promote segregation, nonwhites were divided into categories—Bantu (black Africans) and colored (people of mixed race). Bantu and colored people were not only separated from whites but were also separated from each other in order to weaken their political power.

Even as this was happening, it took Dennis a while before he began to act upon the racial injustice that surrounded him. He would occasionally go to the bookstore in town and ask to see international newspapers like the London *Times* or *The Observer*. The woman behind the counter would say something like, "Tell your master they haven't come in yet." She just assumed a black South African couldn't read English. Dennis found this to be a type of arrogant racism, but it was still not enough to get him to act against it.

What finally did move him to act were a few things that happened around the same time.

First, the **ghetto** just outside Port Elizabeth was declared a white area. Poor blacks who lived in the ghetto were forced out to another ghetto farther from the city. At the same time, government officials were cracking down on schools because they thought the schools were not doing enough to encourage students to accept apartheid. Many of the schools had been run by missionaries, who had the best interest of the children at heart. The government took the schools away from the missionaries. The government's idea of school was to train black children for manual labor jobs.

In the documentary *Dennis Brutus: I Am a Rebel*, Dennis told the story of another moment that led him to a life of activism. He was standing at a non-white bus stop when a police officer came up to a black man who was also waiting for the bus. The officer asked the man for his pass. Under the apartheid regime, blacks and coloreds had to carry with them a pass that identified them as such in order to travel to certain parts of the country. Traveling without a pass put you at risk of arrest or a beating from the police.

The man showed the police officer his pass, and the officer took it and ripped it up.

"Now you don't have a pass," the officer said.

"It was that kind of moment when you felt that

the injustice was so intolerable that you would take a stand," Dennis said.[11]

Teachers were looked up to for leadership, and Dennis helped build a new school in the Port Elizabeth ghetto where blacks had been forced to move. Dennis put a great deal of work into this. He worked with the Education Department to get building permits. He helped fix some plumbing problems. He did a little of everything. The people who put the school together wanted Dennis to be principal, but the government and the Education Department did not allow it. They said it was because he didn't have enough experience, but Dennis believed this was a political decision.

"I was being hit personally and socially and educationally at the same time," Brutus recalled, "and suddenly I plunged into the existing teacher political organization and became an activist in it."[12]

Dennis started getting more involved in the cause. He spoke at public meetings and edited a journal for others who wanted to get involved. He led a protest against the destruction of the ghettos. He took part in protests against the plans to move blacks into smaller ghettos farther away from the towns where they worked.

But the local protests served as the spark for a larger form of protest that may have been brewing somewhere in the back of Dennis's mind for several years. It started with his passion for sports while at the University of Fort Hare. In addition to playing sports while in school, he had attended large sporting events whenever possible. And one thing had become very obvious to him: blacks were being discriminated against.

Dennis recalled witnessing brilliant athletes who were clearly better than the white South Africans who were representing the country in the Olympics and other major sporting events. The athletes Dennis saw were not selected for these big tournaments for no reason other than that they were black.

Dennis started to meet with black athletes and

organizations throughout South Africa. He did this in his spare time, traveling during holidays. He hitchhiked around the country to set up meetings, and talked to black South African athletes about their situations.

In 1958, Dennis helped create the South African Sports Association and served as the group's secretary. He probably could have been the organization's president, but he didn't want that. He felt the president didn't do enough of the real work that needed to be done. It was the secretary who would be keeping track of meetings and writing important letters and documents that would spell out exactly what the organization was trying to accomplish. And so he became the secretary.

The mission of the South African Sports Association was to right the wrongs that apartheid had created for nonwhite athletes in South Africa, but the creation of the organization also had another effect. It signaled to the South African government that Dennis was someone they needed to keep an eye on.

5.
BANNED

As part of its mission, the South African Sports Association tried to meet with all-white sports organizations and ask them to voluntarily change their stance of denying nonwhite athletes the chance to compete at the highest levels of sports. That strategy proved unsuccessful for Dennis and his colleagues.

Meanwhile, the overall situation in the country was getting worse and worse. In 1958, South African Prime Minister Hendrik Verwoerd took apartheid to another level with the start of a policy called "separate development." He divided the black population into ten different Bantu tribes, called Bantustans. By separating the blacks from each other and dividing them into smaller groups, he could claim that the blacks were no longer a majority.

A few years after that, black South Africans were forcibly removed from rural areas that were then sold at extreme discounts to white farmers. Between 1961 and 1994, more than 3.5 million black South Africans were forced to move, and sent to impoverished areas.

Anyone in the country caught protesting or even just meeting to organize opposition to apartheid was arrested for high treason.

More people around the world took notice of what was happening in South Africa on March 21, 1960. After a day of **demonstrations** in the township of Sharpeville, five thousand protesters marched toward the police station. To this day, there is debate as to whether the protesters were peaceful or might have been throwing rocks at the police. Here's what we do know about this event, now known as the Sharpeville Massacre: police opened fire on the crowd, killing sixty-nine people and injuring one hundred eighty others.

The United Nations condemned the act, and governments around the world became more aware of South Africa's apartheid regime. Within South Africa, however, the government took measures to limit internal protest. The massacre led to the banning of the two major organizations that were fighting for the rights of black South Africans—the Pan Africanist Congress (PAC), which had organized the Sharpeville demonstrations, and the African National Congress (ANC).

In 1961, the ANC formed a new branch called the Spear of the Nation. Its leader was a man named Nelson Mandela. Mandela was already a vocal activist and leader in the fight against apartheid. Dennis had met him before and admired what he was doing.

The white government recognized that Mandela

was a serious threat to their way of life. For that reason, Mandela was forced into hiding. For months he was constantly on the move. He even spent some time hiding out in Dennis's house on Shell Street.

"He was so bored because he couldn't leave the house," Dennis recalled years later.[13] As a young man, Mandela had been a successful amateur boxer. To pass the time while hiding out, he taught Brutus's two oldest sons, Marc and Julian, how to box.

After four years of getting nowhere trying to improve nonwhite athletes' opportunities in South Africa, Dennis tried something new in January 1963. The South African Sports Association disbanded, and Dennis helped create a new organization—the South African Non-Racial Olympic Committee (SAN-ROC). This time he did accept the title of president. He was determined to be more than just a figurehead, and met with as many organization leaders throughout Africa as he could to explain why SAN-ROC's mission was so important.

"The Olympics is something which is very dear to me," Dennis said in *Dennis Brutus: I Am a Rebel*, the documentary about his life. "I take it very seriously. It was about idealism and achievement. To go higher, to go faster, to go stronger. These are great ideals. Human perfection, athletic perfection."[14]

The ideals of sports are universal, so Dennis felt strongly that people around the world could at least understand that apartheid created an unfair situation for athletes. Once that was established, it would be easier to shine a light on the real atrocities of South Africa's racial policies.

The South African government also recognized the importance of Dennis's meeting with groups from other countries. What would happen if he partnered with others who thought the South African government's treatment of nonwhites was unfair? They felt threatened by this, and they acted quickly to make it harder for Dennis to accomplish his mission.

The government had a policy in place to deal with

people who opposed them. Dennis received an official banning. He was not allowed to be a member of SAN-ROC or any other organization. He was not allowed to meet with more than two people at a time, not allowed to speak in public, and not allowed to travel outside his hometown.

The ban also meant that Dennis's writing could not be published in South Africa. Until this time, his writing had mostly been articles in journals. He had written some poems that had run in his school magazines, but he was not recognized as a famous poet.

That was about to change.

Dennis's poems could not be published in South Africa, but they were sent to a literary organization in Nigeria, a country in northern Africa that was about three thousand miles from South Africa.

In 1962, Dennis was awarded the Mbari Prize for Poetry. The Mbari Club presented this award every year to a black African poet. Awarding the prize to

Dennis created some controversy. Because he was of mixed race and not solely black, some thought he should not be nominated for the award.

Others, however, pointed to the poems Dennis had written. Some were traditional love poems, but many of them were about the unfair conditions that all nonwhite people in South Africa had to endure. Enough voters believed that Dennis's poetry told the story of all black South Africans. For that reason, he was given the award.

But Dennis did not like the idea that the award was normally restricted to just black poets. As a form of protest, he refused to accept it.

The Mbari Club also *published* books by black African writers. In 1963 they compiled a collection of Dennis's poems and published *Sirens, Knuckles, Boots*.

Dennis had his first printed book of poetry. Sadly, he couldn't see it. *Sirens, Knuckles, Boots* could not be published in South Africa because of his ban. But that didn't really matter to him at the time, as he was focusing on a larger political issue.

Even though he was banned from doing certain things, Dennis was determined to continue his fight against apartheid.

6.
SHOT IN THE BACK

Since the formation of the South African Non-Racial Olympic Committee (SAN-ROC), Dennis had been pushing to get a meeting with the South African National Olympic Committee (SANOC), but his requests were ignored. In May 1963, Dennis heard that SANOC was meeting with a journalist from Switzerland named Rudolph Balsiger. Balsiger was a close associate of the president of the International Olympic Committee, and he was being sent to South Africa to file a report on the rumors of racial discrimination in South African sports.

Dennis's concern was that Balsiger was only meeting with the officials from SANOC, who were all white. One of those officials was a man named Hannes Botha, who had been appointed by the government to make sure that apartheid policies were upheld in sports. How was the International Olympic Committee going to get both sides of this story?

Despite the banning order that prevented him from attending meetings involving more than two people, Dennis felt it was his responsibility to go to the SANOC offices in Johannesburg and try to meet with Balsiger.

When he got there, he was arrested. He was able to post bail and return home after the arrest, but there was little he could do while awaiting trial. He had to check in with police on a daily basis so that they knew he wasn't leaving town.

Still, Dennis was focused on what SAN-ROC should do next. It was clear that the organization could not persuade the South African government and athletic associations to change on their own, so SAN-ROC's strategy changed. They were now going to appeal to the Olympic committees from other countries and persuade them to ban South Africa from the Olympics unless the apartheid government abandoned their system of racial injustice. SAN-ROC hoped that if more countries spoke out, people would be more likely to listen.

Dennis began to have secret contact with the International Olympic Committee (IOC). That contact was long-distance, of course, because he could not leave South Africa. He reached people on the phone when he could, and wrote many letters detailing the situation and asking for help.

As the start of his trial grew near, Dennis knew there was a strong possibility that it would result in him being sent to prison. He considered fleeing the country. In fact, several friends who were involved in the fight against apartheid began planning how it would be done. Dennis understood that fleeing the country would mean he would no longer be able to see May and his children. When he finally agreed to leave South Africa, he knew he had to tell his wife.

May and the kids were in Port Elizabeth, nearly seven hundred miles away from Johannesburg. It was illegal for her to visit her husband while he was awaiting trial, but Dennis applied for and received special permission for May to come see him. He told her of his plans to leave the country, but he refused to give her any details.

"I would not tell her where I was going so that if she were questioned or interrogated or tortured by the secret police, she would simply not have the information to give them," Brutus said in his autobiography.[15]

Dennis had a very specific destination in mind. He wanted to get to Germany for a meeting of the IOC. He got as far as Mozambique, a colony of Portugal about one thousand miles northeast of South Africa. While there, he was detained by Portuguese secret police, who returned him to South African authorities.

Dennis was taken back to Johannesburg, and a sense of desperation overtook him. He feared the police could do whatever they wanted to him and would not let his family know what happened. He was afraid the police would do as they had done during the Sharpeville Massacre three years earlier. When the police car transporting him stopped at the main police station in Johannesburg, his captors instructed him to get his bag from the trunk of the car. Dennis retrieved the bag and set it down on the curb. There was no time to plan his next move, but Dennis knew he did not want to let these police officers bring him in. He started to run!

Dennis led the two police officers who had brought him back to Johannesburg on a chase through the streets of the city. He tried to get on a crowded bus for nonwhites that would have taken him to a ghetto outside city limits, but the bus driver shoved him back onto the street.

As he continued running, one of the officers chasing him shot him in the back.

At first, Dennis didn't realize he'd been shot, and he continued running through the streets of Johannesburg. He got a few more blocks before he finally collapsed on a busy street in the middle of downtown.

An ambulance arrived. Two men got out, took a stretcher from the back of the vehicle, and approached. When they saw Dennis, however, they put the stretcher back into the ambulance and drove away.

"That is an ambulance for whites only," said the officer who shot him. He told Dennis that those men would have lost their jobs if they'd taken him. "You will have to wait for a non-white ambulance."[16]

As Dennis lay on the street, waiting for a colored ambulance to come, he looked up at the tall buildings all around him. He had a sudden realization: the whites in power in South Africa didn't run the country by themselves; they relied on money from other countries. These countries didn't care about apartheid. They weren't concerned about South Africa's social policies. The countries invested in South Africa in order to exploit its resources.

Until that point, Dennis had been focused on the idea that the South African government might change its apartheid system if enough people around the world publicly disagreed with it. Unfortunately, the government didn't seem to care what others thought. But perhaps government officials would care if corporations stopped investing money in South Africa.

Thirty minutes passed before an ambulance for coloreds arrived on the scene. By that time, Dennis had lost a lot of blood. He was taken to the hospital and placed in intensive care, where he received much-needed oxygen. When his wife, May, arrived to see him, she was greeted by security guards who were smoking cigarettes right next to her husband's bed.

They certainly didn't care if smoking next to a patient receiving oxygen was a bad idea. May insisted that they leave the room.

Dennis was in the hospital for twelve days, recovering from the gunshot wound. On September 29, 1963, he was taken to the main prison in Johannesburg to await his sentencing. He was there for more than three months. It wasn't until the first week of January 1964 that the decision was made:

Dennis would serve eighteen months of hard labor in South Africa's most notorious prison—Robben Island.

7.
ROBBEN ISLAND

Robben Island was not much more than a giant slab of rock in the ocean about eight miles off the coast of Cape Town, South Africa. With the hot sun in the summer and cold winds and rain in the winter, life on Robben Island was bleak. In other words, it was a good location for a prison.

Dutch settlers first started sending political prisoners to Robben Island as far back as the seventeenth century. Political prisoners are people who are imprisoned for opposing the government. These prisoners were brought in from Dutch colonies around the world. Three hundred years later it became the place where the white South African government sent vocal and disruptive opponents of apartheid. People like Dennis Brutus.

For prisoners on Robben Island, most of the day was dedicated to the task of breaking large rocks and stones. In theory they were producing gravel that would be used on the mainland. But the primary intention of having the prisoners spend all day chopping rocks was to slowly break their will.

Since Robben Island was a place for political prisoners, Dennis knew several of his fellow inmates. In fact, he was in a cell next to a man he knew well— Nelson Mandela. Mandela had already been a prominent voice in the fight against apartheid when he'd hidden in Dennis's house a few years earlier. He came to Robben Island around the same time that Dennis got there, but he remained long after Dennis was gone. In Mandela's memoir *Conversations with Myself*, Robben Island is described in this way:

Conditions on Robben Island were, for the first years, very harsh. The food was poor, the work was hard, the summers hot, the winters very cold and the warders brutal. Initially only one short letter and one short visit were allowed every six months. Physical suffering was significant; psychological pain was worse. The petty-mindedness of the authorities was unrelenting.[17]

When Dennis and the new group of prisoners arrived at Robben Island, they were marched to their cells and forced to take off their clothes. They were given blankets but not issued any new clothes. They slept on the floor, wrapped in their blankets.

Dennis recalled later that before the new prisoners went to bed that first night, one of the guards told them to be silent, adding, "You think you have come to Robben Island, but you're wrong. You'll find out that you have come to Hell Island."[18]

When Dennis was on Robben Island, there were about eleven hundred political prisoners. There were only about two hundred other prisoners, most of whom had committed murder or some other violent crime. The political prisoners were separated from the other prisoners because the government didn't want people like Dennis to spread their messages of protest and revolution. Talking to one another was not permitted, but Dennis and his fellow prisoners eventually developed a system of gestures to help them communicate. There was a strong bond.

Regardless of the reason why they were on Robben Island, all prisoners had at least one thing in common: they were frequently beaten by the guards, who did not need a reason to do this. The guards definitely did not need any special permission. The ground all around the prison was stained with blood that was drawn by these often-brutal beatings.

In his early days on Robben Island, Dennis thought perhaps he might avoid these attacks if he worked hard and displayed a positive attitude, perhaps even showed a bit of good cheer. Unfortunately for Dennis, this strategy backfired. The number one objective of the guards was to break the spirits of their prisoners. By actually showing some spirit, Dennis drew the wrath of the guards. His body was often badly bruised from the beatings he took.

When they weren't breaking rocks, some prisoners spent time digging limestone out of the quarries. The lime, a mineral that was important for making concrete and other products, was under layers of rock. So the prisoners would have to chip away at the walls of the quarry and then dig out the lime with a shovel. In addition to being hard labor, this work was dangerous for another reason. The glare of the sun reflected off the white limestone directly into the prisoners' eyes. They were not given sunglasses. Many prisoners suffered serious and permanent eye damage.

Another job involved retrieving large stones from

just off the beach, in the shallow waters of the ocean. Dennis was assigned to this job. The rocks were very heavy and often hard to carry because they were slippery from being covered with seaweed.

One day a senior prison officer came to the beach and told the guards that Dennis had applied for permission to continue his studies while in prison, so he deserved "special attention."

That didn't mean he would be allowed to study. "Special attention" meant that now, instead of hauling the stones from beneath the waves, Dennis's job was to push a wheelbarrow that was loaded with the stones. But the load was so heavy that the wheel would sink into the sand. It was almost impossible to move.

Dennis did all he could to push the wheelbarrow, but it would not budge. For that, he was beaten by the guards.

There was nothing to be happy about on Robben Island, but Dennis actually got some good news in the summer of 1964. On August 18, the International Olympic Committee announced that South Africa had been banned from taking part in the Olympic Games that were about to be played in Tokyo, Japan.

The IOC was taking action partly as a result of the efforts by Dennis and the South African Non-Racial Olympic Committee to spread awareness of apartheid around the world. A few months before the Tokyo Olympics, South Africa had received an **ultimatum** from the IOC: the country could compete in the Olympics only if it would **renounce** racial discrimination in sports and end the regulations that banned competition between black and white athletes. When South Africa did not agree to meet these demands, the ban was put into place.

On the day this was announced, Dennis was breaking rocks on Robben Island. As the news spread, he heard it from the guards. It was not possible for him to celebrate this victory while in prison, but this was certainly a significant moment in the fight against apartheid.

While South Africa had not changed any of its discriminatory policies, the Olympic ban at least brought more attention from around the world to what was going on there. The fight, of course, was far from over.

Having visitors on Robben Island was very rare. Only once was May allowed to go to Robben Island to visit her husband. She brought their youngest son, Greg, who was still an infant at the time. But the other children stayed home. May had all the children take turns writing letters to Dennis, but they viewed it as a chore. They did not fully understand why their father was in jail. Sadly, life for them while Dennis was in jail wasn't much different from how it had been beforehand. Dennis had often been too busy to be with them before he'd been sent to Robben Island.

Dennis was prohibited from reading books in

prison, and he was also limited in what he could write. Sometimes he found himself writing poetry on toilet paper. But the most success he had writing poetry during his prison stay was by disguising it in the form of letters. He was afraid that any letters he wrote to his wife would not be private. He expected the guards would read them first, perhaps not even send them. So instead he mailed his poems to his sister-in-law Martha.

In *Letters to Martha*, Dennis refers to "hints of brutality," though he does not come right out and detail any of it. He also refers to the hardships that other prisoners on Robben Island went through:

> ...*the knowledge of those*
> *who endure much more*
> *and endure...*[19]

Of course, there wasn't much to see or do on Robben Island except for the day-to-day life of a prisoner. When it came to **escapism** in Dennis's poetry, there was the occasional reference to birds in the sky:

> *the complex aeronautics*
> *of the birds*
> *and their exuberant aerobatics*
> *become matters for intrigued speculation*
> *and wonderment*[20]

Occasionally Dennis would be sent to solitary confinement, locked in a windowless cell with no connection to anyone or anything outside that tiny space. At first Dennis welcomed this form of punishment. He thought it was an opportunity to just sit and think in quiet solitude. But it didn't take long before he ran out of things to think about. The solitude nearly drove him crazy. That was the purpose of solitary confinement in prison. It was meant to be a severe punishment for prisoners, whether they deserved it or not.

Yet through the mental torture of solitary confinement and the physical torture of hard labor and beatings, Dennis endured. In July 1965, at the end of his eighteen-month sentence, he was released from Robben Island.

Before he left, he made a promise to Mandela that he would continue to do everything in his power to help bring apartheid to an end.

8.
EXILE

When Dennis was released from Robben Island in July 1965, the government did what it could to make sure that he was still not entirely free. He was given a new ban and placed on house arrest.

Not only was he forbidden to meet with more than two people at a time or to speak in public, but he was also not allowed to teach or write. The government wanted to keep Dennis from being able to continue his fight against apartheid.

His oldest child, Jacinta, was fifteen at the

time. Dennis, May, and their seven children were together in their small house on Shell Street in Port Elizabeth. Because Dennis was not permitted to travel, it was actually the most time he had spent with the whole family. But the limitations of the ban made it too difficult for him to be able to work to support them.

With few options left, Dennis applied for and received an exit permit. This document declared that he could leave the country, but on one condition: he could not come back. He didn't want to leave South Africa, but he knew he could do more to fight apartheid from anywhere else. The South African government could not limit his activity once he was out of the country. But the idea that he could never return was a big deal.

He was an **exile**.

It took almost a year before the exit permit was approved, so it wasn't until July 1966 that Dennis left South Africa. His plan was to move to London, where he had friends who were active in trying to bring an end to apartheid.

Dennis arrived in London on the day of the World Cup final, the biggest event in international soccer, which was played in London's Wembley Stadium. One of his friends invited him to the match.

"So there I am in the grandstand at Wembley," Dennis recalled. "And I'm watching with a hundred and ten thousand people in the stadium. The day before, it had been a crime for me to be with more than two people at the same time. So you had this kind of absurd contrast."[21]

Once Dennis was in London, he resumed the work he had started with the South African Non-Racial Olympic Committee. He continued to actively work both to keep South Africa banned from the Olympics and to get countries around the world to stop doing business with his native country until apartheid was defeated.

He also had his family move to be with him. It

would have been easier for May and their children to remain in South Africa, but she wanted to be with her husband. May and the children left South Africa to be with Dennis in England.

But even once the entire family was in England, they did not all live in the same place. Dennis and May did not have much money, so they had to rely on help from friends in order to find shelter. There were people in England working to fight apartheid in South Africa, and they helped. But because the family was so big, the Brutus children had to split up.

Three prominent anti-apartheid activists living in London at the time were Chris de Broglio, Ruth First, and Adelaide Hain. Chris, Ruth, and Adelaide were kind enough to let some of the Brutus kids stay with them. But the three of them were scattered in different parts of the city. It was a very tough time for the Brutus children. London was much colder than South Africa, especially in the winter, and they were unhappy about the weather conditions.

Dennis and May worked at Canon John Collins's Defence and Aid Fund in London. A canon is someone who works for the church. Canon John Collins, who served at St. Paul's Cathedral, was a noted British activist who championed many causes. He first visited South Africa in 1954 and was immediately troubled by the country's policy of racial segregation and **oppression**. From the Defence and Aid Fund, Collins and others worked to raise money around the world to help anti-apartheid activists and political prisoners in South Africa.

Dennis and May both played a part in this. While Dennis traveled and met with leaders around the world and spoke at lectures and conferences about his plight, May helped in letter campaigns. She mailed funds and all manner of support to families in South Africa who were struggling because relatives were awaiting trial or were already in detention. Having gone through that herself, May could certainly identify with those families.

Dennis had been in prison when South Africa had

been banned from the 1964 Summer Olympics, but the mission of achieving equality in sports was not over. Just three years later, South Africa persuaded the International Olympic Committee to lift the ban. The apartheid government still wouldn't allow black athletes to compete against white athletes within South Africa, but they would allow it for competition outside the country's borders.

Most people recognized that this was a very minor concession on the part of the South African government. It would be much harder for black athletes to make South Africa's Olympic team, because they were training with inferior equipment and in inferior facilities. So in a sense, they were still being prevented from competing.

Still, the IOC sent a group of officials to meet with South African officials, and somehow the IOC decided to lift the ban and invite South Africa to the 1968 Summer Olympics in Mexico City.

Dennis was once again ready to use the Olympics

as a way to gain international support for his belief that apartheid was wrong.

He felt strongly that South Africa's Olympic ban should be reinstated. The 1964 ban had raised awareness of apartheid, but nothing had changed. Dennis wanted to continue putting pressure on the South African government.

He had an organized plan to build support for this mission. Stage one was to get all the other African countries united against South Africa. Stage two involved meeting with the Cuban Olympic Committee and with countries in South America. Then Dennis traveled to New Delhi, India, where he got the countries of Asia to unite against South Africa. Next he met with the Soviet Union. The Soviet Union always fielded one of the largest and most successful Olympic teams, so it was big news when Soviet officials told Dennis they would consider boycotting the 1968 Games if South Africa were allowed to participate.

Lastly, Dennis presented his case to Avery Brundage,

an American who was the president of the International Olympic Committee. Dennis explained to Brundage that he had met with all these countries and built a powerful **coalition**. He told Brundage that if South Africa were allowed to participate in the 1968 Olympics, there were ninety countries prepared to **boycott**. That was about 80 percent of all the countries planning to compete.

It was a persuasive argument, to be sure, but Brundage refused to comply. When Dennis recalled this story in *Dennis Brutus: I Am a Rebel*, he was bemused at the response he got from the president of the IOC:

"If I am the only spectator in the stadium, and South Africa is the only team in the Olympics, the Games are still going on."[22]

Clearly there was more work to do. But Dennis was now getting plenty of help from all over the world.

In February 1968 a group of American athletes spoke out in protest of South Africa's being allowed to participate in the 1968 Summer Olympics. Hall of Fame baseball player Jackie Robinson, who broke the color barrier in Major League Baseball in 1947, and basketball star K. C. Jones, who later was enshrined in the Basketball Hall of Fame, issued the following statement on behalf of a long list of athletes from US professional and college sports teams:

> The announced "new policy" in South African sports is a fraud. South Africa is still in violation of the Olympic Charter. The South African proposal is to send a multi-racial team to the Olympics. But this contingent will be selected after four sets of racially segregated trials for Africans, Asians, Coloreds, and Whites. The South African Prime Minister has said, concerning segregation in South Africa, there can be "no **compromise**,

negotiations, or abandonment of principles." This means the practice of segregated sports and spectators will continue. It means that nonwhite athletes must still train with inferior facilities and will not compete in the best stadiums.

If the International Olympic Committee accepts South African **tokenism**, it will appear that international sportsmen condone South Africa's apartheid policy. To the nonwhite majority in South Africa it will be just another indication that the world is willing to compromise with the indignity of white supremacy.

As a member of the National Committee of the American Committee on Africa, I have written to American athletes whom I know to be concerned with the integrity of the Olympics and of American athletics, asking them to join in the following statement:

"I join the protest of the Supreme Council for Sport in Africa against South Africa's participation in the 1968 Olympic Games. Racial discrimination is a violation of the Olympic rules, and South Africa continues to ignore this principle even in her projected 'new sports policy.' This policy reflects the apartheid system which governs all of South African life because, according to the plan, South Africa's Olympic Team would only be selected after separate racial competitions were held for each different racial group. In addition, sports and spectators would continue to be segregated within South Africa. Therefore, South Africa should not be readmitted to the 1968 Olympics."[23]

The interest of fairness was not the only factor that eventually led the IOC to take action against South Africa. By threatening to boycott, countries around the world were shedding a light on the evils of apartheid, but they were also creating a situation that put the host country of the 1968 Olympics, Mexico, in a particularly challenging situation.

Mexico had spent nearly one hundred million dollars to build a new stadium for use in the Olympics. Maybe Brundage didn't care if he were the only person in that stadium, but Mexico would lose massive amounts of money if the stadium weren't filled—which was exactly what would happen if fans were not able to watch their countrymen competing.

Brundage called a meeting of the IOC's executive board on April 21, 1968, after which the IOC recommended that South Africa should not participate in the 1968 Olympics.

Thus, South Africa was banned from the 1968 Summer Olympics. And if the South Africans had any intention of going to the next Olympics, held four years later, they would be disappointed.

The decision to exclude South Africa from the Olympics in 1968 was a result of pressure from what it called the "international climate." After the 1968 ban, the IOC appointed a committee to further investigate the South African Olympic Committee. The IOC's report detailed several allegations of racial discrimination, which was a violation of the Olympic Charter. At its annual conference in 1970, the IOC officially voted to expel South Africa from the Olympics until further notice.

This was a major victory for Dennis. But while the Olympic ban raised international awareness and further isolated South Africa from the world, the apartheid regime continued and Dennis was still an exile.

9.
THOUGHTS ABROAD

Even as Dennis Brutus traveled the world, one thing was certain: he would not be allowed back in South Africa.

Dennis grew to resent it whenever people would ask him what it was like to be an exile, and he was asked the question often. He felt like they were expecting him to feel sorry for himself, to break down and say something like, "Oh, my heart is breaking. I'm cut off from my people."

He may have missed his homeland, but he also

knew that what he was doing was important. And so he could not think of himself as an exile.

"When I was told I could not be a citizen in South Africa, I said, 'I don't need it,'" he explained. "I'm a citizen of the world."[24]

Bernth Lindfors remembers meeting Dennis Brutus for the first time when Dennis was visiting the United States in 1967. Dennis came to the United States to speak and raise awareness about apartheid. Lindfors was a graduate student at the University of California in Los Angeles (UCLA), where Dennis was to speak. Dennis also read some of his poetry at the event.

Lindfors met Dennis after the event and had a chance to interview him. A student of African literature, Lindfors wanted to talk mainly about Dennis's poetry. Not surprisingly, Dennis ended up talking about politics and several other subjects.

"I recall having been impressed not only with his facility for articulating ideas but also with his friendliness and relaxed unpretentiousness," Lindfors wrote in his introduction to Brutus's autobiography. "He was very approachable and seemed to relish engaging conversation."[25]

It was the beginning of a long friendship between the two men.

Two years after that first meeting, Lindfors was teaching at the University of Texas at Austin. As part of his work with the school's Afro-American Studies and Research Center, Lindfors edited a journal called *Research in African Literatures* that he published twice a year and distributed free of charge to anyone interested. The publication was mailed to about two thousand libraries and scholars around the world.

With the institute's approval, Lindfors also published occasional pamphlets that included work from writers who had visited the campus. Dennis Brutus was one such visitor. He came to the University of Texas in 1970, during a break while he was substitute teaching. In addition to visiting an African literature class at Texas that had been studying his poetry, Dennis actually contributed a new book of poetry, *Poems from Algiers*, that the institute published and distributed to its subscribers.

Poems from Algiers consisted of poems that Dennis had written while he'd been at the Pan-African Cultural Festival in Algiers in the summer of 1969. Unlike Dennis's earlier poetry, which was grittier and expressed the anger he felt during his time in prison, *Poems from Algiers* was more a reflection of his life in exile. The poems had a softer tone and expressed a nostalgic feeling about South Africa.

Unfortunately for Dennis, nobody living in South Africa at the time could know how he felt. Not only was Dennis exiled from the country, but censorship laws prevented his work from being published there. It was illegal for a bookstore in South Africa to carry anything written by him.

In the summer of 1970, Dennis and Lindfors came up with a plan to get around this ban. Dennis, while still living in London, gave Lindfors several boxes of his writing—letters, manuscripts, poems—to be saved as part of a collection archived at the University of Texas. Later that year Dennis and Lindfors created their own publishing company, Troubadour Press, and put together a small book of poetry with work from those boxes. But the book, *Thoughts Abroad*, did not have Dennis's name attached. He used a pseudonym—a fake name—as the author. *Thoughts Abroad* by John Bruin was sold in bookstores and carried in libraries throughout South Africa.

The back cover of *Thoughts Abroad* included the following author bio:

> John Bruin is a South African
> currently teaching and writing outside
> his country. He is, as his work shows,
> both widely traveled and homesick.
> He has already been published in
> many magazines, in various countries

and languages, and has a steadily growing reputation as perhaps one of the first South African poets to achieve international recognition. Two books of his poetry are due to appear shortly; for fuller information write to Troubadour Press.[26]

Dennis and Lindfors had quite a bit of fun with their charade. They put out a flyer listing twelve new titles that were due out soon from Troubadour Press—even though they had no intention of publishing any other books. To avoid any trouble, they made it clear in the flyer that people could only order and pay for books that had already been published. John Bruin's *Thoughts Abroad* was the only one.

There was a specific reason why the fake company that published *Thoughts Abroad* was called Troubadour Press. Dennis considered himself a troubadour, which was a title used to describe a type of wandering singer during the Middle Ages in France. A troubadour was both a poet and a knight, who fought to protect a loved one from injustice. In the case of Dennis, his loved one was his country.

When Dennis was awaiting trial after his arrest in 1963, he wrote one of his most famous poems, "A Troubadour, I Traverse . . ." It was later published as part of a collection of his poems in 1973.

A troubadour, I traverse all my land
exploring all her wide-flung parts with zest . . .

and I have laughed, disdaining those who banned
inquiry and movement, delighting in the test
of will when doomed by Saracened arrest,
choosing, like unarmed thumb, simply to stand.
Thus, quixoting till a cast-off of my land
I sing and fare, person to loved-one pressed
braced for this pressure and the captor's hand

that snaps off service like a weathered strand:
—no mistress-favour has adorned my breast
only the shadow of an arrow-brand.[27]

In this poem Dennis refers to "those who banned" him, testing his will and arresting him. The "unarmed thumb" refers to a raised thumb, which was a symbol of the anti-apartheid movement. The "weathered strand" refers to Robben Island, the prison where Dennis was sent not long after he wrote this poem. While some troubadours might wear a scarf or something else belonging to their wives when they go into battle, Dennis preferred to wear a prison outfit. The "arrow-brand" refers to the arrow on an old-fashioned prison uniform.

There were one thousand copies of *Thoughts Abroad* printed. Some actually sold, helping to cover the cost of putting this project together. Most of the books, however, were sent directly to Dennis's friends and former colleagues in South Africa.

The publication of *Thoughts Abroad* was a plot designed to trick the South African government and sidestep its censorship laws, and John Bruin was a fictitious author. But the poems in *Thoughts Abroad* were real, and it might not have been hard for someone familiar with Dennis Brutus's poetry to read this book and feel that it related to Dennis.

10.
COMING
TO AMERICA

Because of apartheid, South Africa had been banned from the Olympics. But Dennis Brutus did not stop using sports as a way to increase awareness of apartheid. He remained focused on the idea that sports could be a powerful tool for protest.

"Very often, the people who ran sport were also very powerful people in the government and in the corporations," he said. "So you were really up against the British establishment at an aristocratic level."[28]

To gain attention, Dennis even protested at one of

the most prestigious sporting events in the world—the championship of the All England Lawn Tennis Club, also known as Wimbledon.

Wimbledon is one of the four major world events in professional tennis. It is not uncommon for celebrities and dignitaries and even members of England's royal family to attend. Now that Dennis was in England himself, it was time for him to make his Wimbledon debut. Since there would be an international audience, this would be an important opportunity to spread his anti-apartheid message.

Dennis attended Wimbledon on the second day of the 1971 championships, taking a seat in the stands during a doubles match on Court 2. After the second point in the second set, Dennis got out of his seat, walked onto the court, and blew a whistle. He handed out leaflets to the four players, to the linesmen, to the ball boys, and finally to the umpire.

His message: Wimbledon was wrong for allowing white South Africans to compete in the tournament, because of South Africa's unfair treatment of black athletes.

By the time he had handed out his leaflets, the police had arrived. Dennis lay down on the court, so the officers literally had to drag him away. He was arrested, though the charges were later dropped. Not surprisingly, this was reported on the evening news throughout England.

Vincent Moloi, during the course of filming a documentary about Dennis, came to understand why using sports as a platform for protest was so effective.

"I was realizing the genius of Dennis choosing sport as a vehicle for struggle," Moloi said. "Dennis was arguing for fair play on the sports field, a time-honored place of equality and impartiality."[29]

During his five years living in England as an exile, Dennis Brutus had several opportunities to visit the United States, usually for speaking engagements, poetry readings, or to participate in some kind of protest. Sometimes the occasion would be a combination of all three.

In 1970, Dennis had an extended stay in America when he was invited to be a guest professor at the University of Denver. The school needed a substitute for its African literature professor, who was taking a semester off. It made perfect sense that they called Dennis, because the professor he would be sitting in for was Zeke Mphahlele. Just like Dennis, Mphahlele was a South African teacher and writer who had been exiled from his native land. Mphahlele had been fired from his job as a teacher in South Africa for opposing segregation in the schools, and he had left South Africa permanently in 1957, nine years before Dennis.

Dennis enjoyed his time teaching at the University of Denver, though he returned to Britain after the semester was over.

A year later, in September 1971, he was offered a position in the English Department at Northwestern

University in Evanston, Illinois. He accepted the job, and moved to the United States.

Three of his children came with him to the United States in 1971. His wife, May, and his other kids joined them a year later. Two of his children, Tony and Tina, went to college in the States. Tony went to Harvard; Tina attended Grinnell College. May, however, was not happy in the United States. She preferred living in England. After a year in the States, she and six of their children returned to London.

Dennis would have preferred to be with his wife and kids, but he understood May's desire to be in England. It was certainly not the first time he'd been separated from his family. Unlike when he'd been in prison, though, this separation was his choice. He wanted to stay in America at this time, even if his family didn't.

When Dennis came to live in the United States, he often wondered how he was perceived by black South Africans still suffering under apartheid rule. Did they think he was enjoying his freedom in America? Did they think he was no longer concerned with the plight of others?

It's doubtful that anyone who knew what Dennis stood for would think that. If they did, however, Dennis was given the opportunity to send them a message in 1971.

It was near the beginning of his time teaching African Literature at Northwestern. One day he heard the news that Catherine Taylor, a white South African woman who was a member of South Africa's Parliament, was going to be a guest lecturer on campus. It was his understanding that Taylor was there to speak about how Africans in general were accepting the apartheid system.

Nearly fifteen years before the formation of Northwestern's Anti-Apartheid Alliance, Dennis helped organize a takeover of the lecture. Taylor was encouraged to go back to South Africa and let her compatriots know how Americans felt about apartheid. The story was covered by South African press, and Dennis was identified as one of the key voices of protest.

Dennis was delighted about the idea that South Africans could see that he was still politically active. Just as important, he was glad that Northwestern's administration was not concerned with his involvement in the protest. He realized his employer would not restrain him from his activism.

That was not the only time he had a chance to continue his activism. In 1973, Brutus was invited to a convention of the United Church of Christ in Saint Louis, Missouri. The lead speaker at this convention was Chief Gatsha Buthelezi, who was the prime minister of the most important Bantustan in South Africa.

Bantustans were the tribes created in 1958 by the white South African government to split up South Africa's black population.

Buthelezi had achieved an important status in South Africa because he did not fight the apartheid regime. Dennis made it clear at the convention that Buthelezi did not speak for the majority of black South Africans.

When Buthelezi returned to South Africa, he called a press conference in which he criticized Dennis. But when this news spread, it actually made Dennis look good in the eyes of black South Africans. They were reminded that Dennis was speaking out on their behalf far away in the United States.

While he was teaching at Northwestern, Dennis also continued his role as an activist and a "citizen of the world." In 1974, for instance, he traveled to Dar es Salaam in the African country of Tanzania for a meeting of the Pan Africanist Congress. The African National Congress (ANC) had invited him to be a delegate for them at the meeting.

The real reason he went to Dar es Salaam, however, was that there was another big meeting taking place in the city at around the same time. Dennis attended a meeting of the FIFA Congress. FIFA is the international governing body for soccer (known as football in most of the world). Working with the African delegates, he succeeded in getting FIFA to ban the South African Football Association from international soccer events.

The FIFA World Cup is one of the biggest sporting events in the world. Like the Olympics, it takes place every four years. And now, like the Olympics, it was banning South Africa from competing because of apartheid.

11.
DENNIS BRUTUS DEFENSE COMMITTEE

Dennis Brutus kept the promise he'd made to Nelson Mandela, who was still a prisoner on Robben Island when Dennis came to America in 1971. Dennis continued to speak out against South Africa's apartheid rule every chance he could.

Mandela was becoming a major symbol around the world. There was nothing he could do to fight apartheid while he was in prison, but many others did their part.

One such freedom fighter was a South African

named Stephen Biko. In the 1960s and '70s, Biko was one of the leaders of an anti-apartheid group called the Black Consciousness Movement (BCM). As the BCM grew, the government considered it a threat. In 1973, Biko received a banning order.

Biko could not leave his home township, and he was forbidden to speak in public or talk to the media. But in 1977 he violated the banning order. He traveled to Cape Town in hopes of meeting with some members of the BCM.

On his way home from Cape Town, Biko was detained by police. He remained in custody for three weeks. He was interrogated and beaten multiple times. The beatings eventually killed him.

More than twenty thousand people attended Biko's funeral. Like Mandela, he became an international symbol of the anti-apartheid movement. In the coming years, more and more countries began to put pressure on South Africa to end apartheid.

• • •

Biko's death was a reminder that it was unsafe for anyone to speak out against apartheid in South Africa. Dennis Brutus couldn't return home to South Africa even if he wanted to. It was too dangerous.

As a vocal opponent of apartheid, Dennis was considered an enemy of the government. A former South African agent said that his government rated Dennis "one of the twenty most dangerous South African political figures overseas."[30] Dennis believed that anywhere he might travel on the African continent, he could be assassinated.

So it literally became a matter of life or death when Dennis was informed of some news in 1980. He was told that a technicality regarding his passport might force him to leave the United States and return to Africa.

Since Dennis had been born in Southern Rhodesia, which was a British colony at the time, he always had a British passport. He'd been permitted to travel with the British passport.

In 1980, Rhodesia gained independence from

Britain and became Zimbabwe. This meant that Dennis would need a new passport, issued from Zimbabwe, in order to be allowed to travel outside Zimbabwe.

Getting a new passport would take some time, but US officials didn't give Dennis that time. They ordered him to leave the country. Fearing for his life if he returned to Africa, Dennis filed court papers to seek political **asylum** in America.

Political asylum is a form of protection that a country can offer a person if that person believes his or her political beliefs would make it dangerous for them to return home. In Dennis's case, the protection he was seeking was simply the right to stay in the United States.

His case was an international news story. Chester Crocker, the United States' assistant secretary of state for African Affairs, appeared on ABC's news program *Nightline*, to defend the US government's position.

"Mr. Brutus is being treated like anybody else,"

Crocker said. "We have laws, and they must be applied."[31]

There have always been exceptions and special circumstances, however. Those who supported Dennis's campaign for asylum believed he should be one of the exceptions.

A group called the Dennis Brutus Defense Committee was formed to help Dennis raise money and gain support for a legal battle that would last two years. The US Immigration and Naturalization Service was intent on having Dennis deported. The Dennis Brutus Defense Committee, led by several members of the Northwestern University faculty and some prominent political figures, including future Chicago mayor Harold Washington, gathered thirty thousand names of people who supported Dennis's right to gain asylum in America. In papers the committee filed, it stated that "if deported, Dennis Brutus will become a target of assassination for the South African secret police, because of the lifelong battle he has waged against racism and apartheid."[32]

Dennis himself pointed out news of Joe Gqabi, a former nationalist leader in South Africa who had been in prison on Robben Island with him. Gqabi had been gunned down, killed in his driveway in a suburb of Salisbury, Zimbabwe. The prime minister of Zimbabwe, Robert Mugabe, had accused South Africa of the assassination.

The judge hearing the case was convinced that Dennis's life would be in danger if he was sent back to Africa. In September 1983, after a two-year battle in the courts, Brutus was officially granted political asylum in the United States.

He stayed another two years at Northwestern before taking a job as professor of both English and African Studies at the University of Pittsburgh, and he continued to speak at other schools around the country. By the end of the 1980s, he had received a number of awards, as well as other special recognition for his work.

Dennis received honorary degrees from three different colleges in the state of Massachusetts: Worcester State College, the University of Massachusetts–Amherst, and Northeastern University.

In 1987 he was presented with the Langston Hughes Award by the City University of New York. Langston Hughes was a poet and activist who was celebrated for depicting the African American experience in his writing.

And in 1989, Dennis received the Paul Robeson Award, to honor Dennis's artistic excellence, political consciousness, and integrity. Paul Robeson was a very important figure in African American history. He'd been an actor and a singer active in many social and political causes.

Like Robeson and Hughes, Dennis was finally being recognized by more people as a role model, a successful artist who used his status to help inspire and empower others.

12.
END OF
APARTHEID

By the late 1980s, the pressure on South Africa's government to end apartheid was enormous. Much of it was the result of young people in colleges and universities around the world organizing anti-apartheid groups and holding protests.

Dennis Brutus and other prominent anti-apartheid activists had helped spread the word that many colleges were investing millions of dollars in companies that did business in South Africa.

"Divest!"

This was the message that students were sending to their schools' administrators: instead of investing money in companies that did business in South Africa, they should divest—take their money away from those companies.

If money weren't being invested in these companies, explicitly because they were doing business in South Africa, then the companies would be forced to leave that country. If big companies moved out of South Africa, the country's economy would suffer greatly. If apartheid were the reason for this divestment, then well . . . something would have to be done. South Africa would be forced to rethink its policy.

There was another common message being delivered at all the anti-apartheid protests: "Free Nelson Mandela!"

Mandela, a political prisoner for three decades, had become the face of the movement. He was so important, in fact, that high-ranking members of the South African government started to schedule secret meetings with him in prison. The two sides met occasionally for four years, but very little progress was made. That changed in 1989, when South Africa got a new leader.

That was the year that F. W. de Klerk replaced P. W. Botha as president of South Africa. One of the first big decisions he made was to end the ban against the African National Congress and other organizations that had been banned because they opposed apartheid. Next, de Klerk announced that he would release from prison the head of the African National Congress—Nelson Mandela.

There was still much work to be done in order to undo the apartheid policies of South Africa's government and make it a true democracy. De Klerk and the National Party, which was the political party that had been in power since the start of apartheid, continued to meet with the African National Congress and several other groups to negotiate peace.

The rest of the world took notice. In 1991 the

International Olympic Committee lifted its ban and allowed South Africa to compete at the 1992 Olympics in Barcelona, Spain. It was the country's first appearance in the Olympics in thirty-two years.

Three years later, in 1994, the country held a democratic election. The African National Congress defeated the National Party by a wide margin. Mandela, after being in prison for twenty-seven years, was the new president. He was the first black president of South Africa!

Mandela's release and the end of apartheid meant a lot of things to a lot of people. For Dennis Brutus, it meant the chance to end his time as an exile. One condition of his exile in 1966 had been that he would be arrested immediately if he ever returned to South Africa. But now he could request a "letter of indemnity" from the new government. When he received this letter, it eliminated the conditions of his exile. He could return to South Africa anytime he wanted.

Perhaps even more important than that, the end

of apartheid also meant that all of Dennis's books of poetry would finally be allowed on bookshelves in South Africa. This made him extremely happy.

Considering the fact that Dennis had used sports to bring awareness to the apartheid problem, it was interesting to see a sporting event become the symbol of apartheid's end.

South Africa got to host the 1995 Rugby World Cup, but there was a big question about how it would play out. There was still racial unrest. Would black South Africans cheer for a national team that was still mostly white?

South Africa's rugby team, the Springboks, were not good enough to qualify for the World Cup based on merit. But they received an automatic bid because South Africa was the host country. Nobody expected them to do very well.

What happened next was incredible. The Springboks shocked the world and reached the championship match. Mandela attended the match wearing a green-and-gold Springbok jersey as a sign of unity. The fans backed their nation's team—and the Springboks won! There was Mandela after the final match, handing his country's rugby team the World Cup trophy!

Mandela's support for the team raised spirits for both blacks and whites in South Africa. Going forward, the expectation was that more black athletes would have a chance to play for the Springboks. For now, they could celebrate the team's victory together.

Still, just because apartheid was over didn't mean everything was perfect. Even after Mandela took power, there were signs of inequality.

Dennis was among a small group of activists who thought Mandela and the African National Congress did not demand enough when they negotiated the end of apartheid. For so many years, blacks and other people of color in South Africa had been kept down, moved out of their homes, and forced to live in poverty.

After apartheid ended, a majority of blacks in South Africa were too poor to enjoy their new-found freedom. Dennis felt some members of the African National Congress were just happy to be in a position of power, so they stopped fighting for all the people.

Dennis also thought that his personal method of protesting apartheid—sports—was being compromised. He was not happy that the International Olympic Committee invited South Africa to the 1992 Games. Black athletes were still at a disadvantage because they had been stuck with inferior equipment and facilities for so long.

"Those are the things that Dennis Brutus was fighting against," Zakes Mda, a professor of creative writing at Ohio University, recalled later. "Those are the things that then he *continued* to fight against, even after apartheid, because you see, unlike many of his comrades—who then of course after apartheid, then they became big shots in the government and so on and then began to enjoy the fruits of liberation . . . he continued to stay outside the system and to fight against his former comrades. . . . Up to the very year that he died, he was involved in a number of activities."[33]

13.
THE POETRY OF DENNIS BRUTUS

The poetry of Dennis Brutus was already well known in literary circles before apartheid ended in 1994. When his books were finally permitted to be read and sold in his native South Africa, there was a new-found appreciation for his work.

It is impossible to separate Dennis Brutus the poet from Dennis Brutus the **civil rights** activist. Everything that he experienced in his life—fighting apartheid, being jailed and tortured, being exiled from his country—naturally shaped his art.

He was not alone. Whether it was poetry, short stories, or novels, almost all South African literature during this period was a reflection of the troubled times.

Dennis's poetry has been praised by critics for its gentle rage. In his most powerful poems, readers can feel his anger and frustration, but they don't feel like they are being yelled at. In *The Chosen Tongue*, Gerald Moore described the challenge of the African poet in general, with particular praise for Dennis.

"Though he must be angry, he must never be shrill," Moore wrote. "His must be a quiet voice where there is already too much shouting. For it is not so much the call to action that he is uniquely qualified to give, as the call to see, to hear and to know. The coloured poet Dennis Brutus has measured the difficulty of this task. . . . He has achieved in some poems a control which masters horror without diminishing its impact."[34]

Of the twelve books of poetry written by Dennis, only one came out before he was imprisoned on

Robben Island. *Sirens, Knuckles, Boots* was published in 1963. That was one year after the government's banning meant that Dennis could not publish written material in the country. For that reason, *Sirens, Knuckles, Boots* was published in Nigeria.

Some of the poems in *Sirens, Knuckles, Boots* were actually love poems that Dennis originally wrote for women he had dated. He realized when he first wrote them that he could craft a poem that contained a private, personal message and make it a public statement as well.

"Many of the love lyrics are also political, if one would read them that way," Dennis would explain in his autobiography. "And many of the political poems are in fact couched in intimate, personal terms."[35]

Whether personal or political, it's clear that Dennis's poetry reflects the struggles of apartheid and the perils that he had to endure. That much is easy to understand just by looking at the titles of his books:

*Sirens, Knuckles, Boots . . . Stubborn Hope . . . Salutes
and Censures . . . Still the Sirens.*

In "Voices Out of the Skull: A Study of Six African
Poets," Paul Theroux expressed his appreciation for
Dennis's work:

> Brutus is whipped and he lashes back
> furiously. It is true that sometimes
> his punches are wild, sometimes he
> misses, but he swings enough times
> for us to see what he is aiming at.[36]

In 1973, Dennis published a new book of poems.
Some were poems he had written years earlier, but he
wanted to add a few new ones. He wanted to write
a poem that would also be the title of this book, one
that captured the theme of his poetry. The poem and
the book are titled *A Simple Lust*. He said the title
referred to a thought he had after an encounter with
a fellow prisoner on Robben Island.

Dennis explained that he was talking to an eighteen-year-old prisoner who had just arrived and was serving a sixty-year sentence. "You know, I am going to be seventy-eight when I leave prison," the man said.

Dennis went back to his cell that night and thought about the young man's situation. Like so many of the political prisoners on Robben Island, the man was there because he had opposed his country's government. He was willing to endure hard labor in jail rather than give up his freedom outside of jail.

"A simple lust is all my woe." That's how the title poem begins. A lust is a desire or a feeling of longing. Dennis explained that his poem refers to a lust for freedom.

> *Only I speak the others' woe;*
> *those congealed in concrete*
> *or rotting in rusted ghetto-shacks;*
> *only I speak their wordless woe,*
> *their unarticulated simple lust.*[37]

"We will die if we can't be free," Dennis said when speaking of this poem. "The poem is about that need, which I call an appetite or a lust, and so the poem is really about the simple lust to be free. And that my poetry speaks about it on behalf of those who cannot speak for themselves."[38]

Dennis had four books of poetry published in the 2000s, long after apartheid had been abolished. The fact that he was still writing poetry was a sign that he was still angry about something. In 2004 he turned eighty years old. He was angry about black South Africans of all ages still living in poverty. He was angry about big companies that weren't sharing their wealth. And he was angry about governments around the world not doing enough to address the dangers of climate change.

In his autobiography Dennis explained that anger was one of the big reasons why he wrote poetry.

"When I am very angry or frustrated and I don't want to get mad—because then I would lose a grip on the situation—I turn inwards, and I write poetry instead, rather than blowing my top."[39]

In 2008, Dennis was awarded the Lifetime Honorary Award by the South African Department of Arts and Culture for his lifelong dedication to African and world poetry and literary arts.

"Brutus was arguably Africa's greatest and most influential modern poet after Leopold Sedar Senghor and Christopher Okigbo," said Olu Oguibe, a writer and artist from Nigeria. "That Brutus was one of the greatest writers of all time, there is no doubt, but he was also an indefatigable campaigner for justice, a relentless organizer, an incorrigible romantic, and a great humanist, and the power and beauty of his spirit and his work will remain with us for long."[40]

14.
RETURN TO SOUTH AFRICA

Dennis continued to teach at the University of Pittsburgh after apartheid was over, but he began making frequent trips back to South Africa. He was a guest lecturer at the University of KwaZulu-Natal in eastern South Africa, and he became involved in many grassroots causes. If he felt something was unfair and there were people suffering because of that unfairness, he couldn't stop himself from speaking out.

He was seventy-five years old when he retired from Pittsburgh in 1999. Still, he never imagined himself growing old, sitting on a park bench, talking to friends and just passing the time away. That would be too boring. More important, he could never just sit and relax when there were injustices around the world.

By 2002, Dennis had returned to South Africa permanently. His wife, May, joined him. She returned from England along with some of their children, all of whom were adults by then. Some had started their own families and chose to stay where they were. They were scattered around the world— England, China, America. Sadly, as was the case for most of their lives, they did not see much of their father even after he retired.

Dennis resided in Cape Town, but even in his eighties, he continued to travel the world to speak out and support any causes he felt were important. The continuing poverty of blacks in South Africa was one of these causes.

"We're in a world now where, in fact, wealth is

concentrated in the hands of a few; the mass of the people are still poor," he told the independent news program Democracy Now! in 2005.[41]

He still thought there should be **reparations**. This is the idea that people who suffered as a result of the apartheid policies should be given money or other benefits to help repair the damage that was done.

Dennis thought the government of South Africa could do more to help, but he wanted others to contribute as well. He felt that big corporations that had invested so much money in South Africa during the time of apartheid also needed to pay up. Many of these companies were from the United States. Dennis argued that they had gotten rich doing business with South Africa even though they'd known that the country's system of apartheid was wrong. Dennis encouraged legal action against these companies, to sue for reparations. He felt that black South Africans had a right to ask these companies for money.

In 2008, Dennis visited the United States to

speak to a group of union workers in Philadelphia who were concerned about working conditions in factories, and he talked about what he had done in the anti-apartheid movement, as well as about the importance of using sports as a stage for protest on a more widespread scale.

"I want to remind you . . . of the many people in the United States in the field of sport who took a stand on issues of human rights," he said.[42] He brought up Tommie Smith and John Carlos, the two African American track stars who had raised their fists—a symbol at the time known as the "Black Power salute"—during a medal ceremony at the 1968 Summer Olympics. He brought up Muhammad Ali, who had given up his heavyweight boxing title because he opposed the Vietnam War and refused to fight. He brought up Arthur Ashe, who had fought for racial equality in tennis.

"In many issues, I'm glad to say, sports people have responded to the issue of human rights," he said.

"And it seems to me we have to build on that and do as much as we can to develop awareness, both on the question broadly of sweatshops and working conditions, but more particularly also on the issue of human rights."[43]

Right up until the year he died, Dennis spoke out for what he believed in. One of the causes he felt strongest about in his later years was that of climate change. On his eighty-fifth birthday in 2009, just a few days before the United Nations Climate Change Conference in Copenhagen, Denmark, he spoke about the importance of protest as a way for people to get their message heard.

With TV news cameras rolling, he told his fellow protesters that these gatherings needed to continue in order to get the message across.

"From now on this is going to be . . . a part of the challenge to the greedy corporate powers that don't care what happens to the planet," he said. "So we expect them to pay attention. We hope that we ourselves will pay attention, and then, most difficult of all, we are going to have to join that struggle. But [there is] not enough time. We are in serious difficulty all over the planet. We are going to change the world. There's too much profit, too much greed, too much suffering by the poor. It has to stop. The planet must be in action. The people of the planet must be in action."[44]

Once again, Dennis was leading the way for a new generation of freedom fighters. Perhaps some at the Copenhagen Climate Change Conference didn't even realize this man had been in prison with Mandela more than forty years earlier.

Patrick Bond, who was the director for the Centre for Civil Society at the University of KwaZulu-Natal in South Africa, had become good friends with Dennis when the two had worked together at the university. After Dennis's death, Bond talked about him in an obituary that aired on the international news program Democracy Now!

"The role that Dennis Brutus played, especially

upon returning to South Africa after democracy in 1994 and living there full-time for the last five years, [was] a really formidable, inspiring role for a new generation of people concerned about inequality and environmental degradation," Bond said.[45]

Throughout the 2000s, Dennis was an annual speaker at the World Social Forum, a meeting of social justice groups from around the world that were committed to shedding light on global issues that the groups could unite to support or oppose.

Of course, Dennis continued to be suspicious of the giant financial organizations, believing their greed and desire to keep all the money in the hands of the rich minority was a form of global apartheid. He could almost always be found at demonstrations opposing global groups like the World Trade Organization, the World Bank, and the International Monetary Fund.

Bond praised Dennis's ability to focus on future concerns without forgetting the past. Even as Dennis got involved with climate change and other current issues, he never stopped reminding the world of the evils that his country had endured.

"He had this extraordinary ability to do the whole spectrum of social struggles—history and future," said Bond. "And to do it with such grace, eloquence, and culture."[46]

15.
THE LEGACY OF DENNIS BRUTUS

On December 26, 2009, Dennis died of complications from prostate cancer.

His family released the following statement upon his death:

"Dennis lived his life as so many would wish to, in service to the causes of justice, peace, freedom and the protection of the planet. He remained positive about the future, believing that popular movements will achieve their aims."[47]

His family understood that Dennis had been

committed to a cause much greater than them. For his part, Dennis had understood that he was not always around for his wife and children. It was a sacrifice by all involved.

Dennis talked about this in the documentary *Dennis Brutus: I Am a Rebel.*

"I had to make a choice fairly early on whether I was going to serve the larger society or whether I would choose to serve them and, of course, neglect the larger issues," Dennis said. "My wife did not oppose the choice. She reminds me now that if she had opposed me, I would anyway have gone ahead. She may be right about that."[48]

We will never know if his wife really was okay with Dennis's choice, but his children definitely recognized that their father was not there for them when they were young. As they got older, they understood the important work Dennis had done all his life, but it didn't mean they were happy that he hadn't been there for them as they were growing up.

"Dennis was on a mission, a crusade, and that drove him above all else," Tony Brutus said of his father.[49]

Dennis was the first to admit that he often was not around for his children. He addressed it in a poem he wrote called "For My Sons and Daughters." This was the verse that he most hoped they would understand:

> *My continual sense of sorrow*
> *drove me to work*
> *and at times I hoped*
> *to shape your better world.*[50]

After his death, the University of KwaZulu-Natal's Centre for Civil Society posted a memorial to Dennis online. In it was a link to a sixty-eight-page document of testimonials—tributes to Dennis from notable people and organizations. Among them was this statement from Archbishop Desmond Tutu, the famed South African cleric who won the 1984 Nobel Peace Prize:

When we needed the support of the
international community to end the
vicious system of racial oppression
called apartheid, we had to have
eloquent advocates to tell the world
our story and persuade it to come to
our assistance. We had none more
articulate than Brutus, our wonderful
poet-campaigner. We owe him an
immense debt of gratitude.[51]

This was the official statement from the South
African government:

[His] contribution to the struggle
against apartheid and passion for
social justice and human rights for all
mankind has left an indelible mark
in South Africa and the international
community. As we celebrate his

lifework as a South African poet and
political activist let us remember that
Brutus's poetic license was first and
foremost inspired by the quest for
the restoration of human dignity and
achievement of a better life for all.[52]

The South African government oppressed Dennis
for so many years. It was the apartheid government
that put him in jail and then forced him to leave the
country. When apartheid ended, the government
completely changed. The fact that it was the government now praising Dennis in this way shows just
how much South Africa has changed. Dennis knew
that in order to achieve a better life for all, protest was
necessary. He was never afraid to get arrested—he
was arrested many times for protesting and standing
up for what he believed was right. As he explained in
Dennis Brutus: I Am a Rebel, the key to successful protest was getting a large number of people who were

willing to give up their freedom for the right cause.

"It's not about me," he said. "It's about millions of people getting arrested. It's about people willing to break the law in order to say, 'We believe in justice and we are opposed to injustice.'"[53]

In 2007, Dennis's lifelong fight for justice seemingly earned him a special honor. Although he had never been a competitive athlete himself, he was voted into the South African Sport Hall of Fame. But Dennis refused the honor, saying that some of its members were "unapologetic racists."[54]

After all, the Hall of Fame had existed long before apartheid had ended. Yet the Hall of Fame had never shared Dennis's interest in pursuing racial equality in sports.

"The equality that he fought for in sports, he still could not see it," observed Ohio University professor Zakes Mda.[55]

This was Dennis's statement in turning down the honor:

"It is incompatible to have those who championed racist sport alongside its genuine victims. It's time—indeed long past time—for sports truth, apologies and reconciliation."[56]

Some people, like documentary filmmaker Vincent Moloi, feel that Dennis does not get the recognition he deserves for his part in the anti-apartheid movement, especially for his role in getting South Africa banned from the Olympics.

"I see this as an incredible achievement in the fight against apartheid, and yet he's not celebrated as a hero of the struggle," Moloi states in his film about Brutus. "I keep on having the feeling that some prominent people have ignored his contribution in the struggle, especially the Olympics."

In the film, Moloi asks Dennis if he thinks his place in history might be overlooked. It should come as no surprise that Dennis, who was always selfless, was not bothered by this idea.

"I really don't feel strongly about it," he said.

"There are people who know that I made a contribution and have either not admitted it or in some cases actually suppressed it. How do I feel about it? Not particularly strongly either way. It's their choice. And of course one doesn't do things in order to be recognized. You do them because they happen to be important."[57]

Dennis Brutus didn't do the things he did as an anti-apartheid activist to gain popularity or to become a leader of people. He was an honest man who fought for fairness and equality. Along the way, though it may not have been his ultimate goal, he did inspire others to do the right thing.

"I think I speak to power, in a sense that I will say what I think is honest even if it makes me unpopular," he said. "Now, if that inspires other young people to say, 'Hey, I am going to speak out,' if it does that, then I'm really pleased."[58]

Glossary

activism the use of direct, often controversial action, such as a demonstration or a strike, in opposition to or support of a cause

apartheid an official policy of racial segregation formerly practiced in South Africa, involving political, legal, and economic unfair treatment of nonwhites

asylum protection from arrest given to political refugees by a nation or by an embassy or other agency

autobiography a history of a person's life, written by himself or herself

ban to prevent someone from doing something

boycott to refuse to have dealings with a person, organization, or country as an expression of protest

civil rights legal rights that all citizens have to make sure they are treated equally

GLOSSARY

coalition a temporary alliance of distinct groups, people, or states for joint action

colony a group of people living in a new territory but continuing their connection with the parent nation

compromise a settlement of differences that is reached by each side giving the other something it wants

demonstration a public display of group feelings toward a person or cause

discrimination unfair treatment of people because of their race, gender, religion, or other personal characteristic

divest to withhold something or take something back, especially property or money

escapism to seek distraction or mental diversion from unpleasant realities

exile a person who is forced to leave his or her country or home

ghetto a part of a city in which members of a minority group live, typically because of social, legal, or economic pressure

missionary related to the work of a religious organization and its efforts to spread its faith or promote human welfare and social reform

oppression the unjust or cruel exercise of authority or power

protest an organized public demonstration of disapproval

racism the belief that one race of people is better than another

renounce to give up by formal declaration

reparations the act of making amends for a wrong that has been done, by paying money to or otherwise helping those who have been wronged

segregation the separation of a certain group so that they have to live in a restricted area and have limited opportunities, separate schools, and other limitations

tokenism the practice of making only a symbolic effort

ultimatum a final proposition, condition, or demand

Endnotes

1   Lewis, "Case for Asylum." *New York Times*, August 25, 1983.

2   Brutus, *Dennis Brutus Tapes*, 35.

3   Brutus, *Dennis Brutus Tapes*, 40.

4   Brutus, *Dennis Brutus Tapes*, 128.

5   Brutus, *Dennis Brutus Tapes*, 145.

6   Brutus, *Dennis Brutus Tapes*, 145.

7   Brutus, *Dennis Brutus Tapes*, 131.

8   Brutus, *Dennis Brutus Tapes*, 137.

9   Brutus, *Dennis Brutus Tapes*, 134.

10   Brutus, *Dennis Brutus Tapes*, 134.

11   Moloi, *I Am a Rebel*.

12   Brutus, *Dennis Brutus Tapes*, 135.

13   Field, "Brutus Helps Hide Mandela."

14   Moloi, *I Am a Rebel*.

15   Brutus, *Dennis Brutus Tapes*, 51.

16   Brutus, *Dennis Brutus Tapes*, 76.

17   Mandela, *Conversations with Myself*, 128.

18   Brutus, *Dennis Brutus Tapes*, 93.

19   Brutus, *Letters to Martha and Other Poems from a South African Prison*, 54.

20   Brutus, *Letters to Martha and Other Poems from a South African Prison*, 66.

ENDNOTES

21   Moloi, *I Am a Rebel*.

22   Moloi, *I Am a Rebel*.

23   Robinson and Jones, "Protesting South Africa's Readmission," 1–2.

24   Moloi, *I Am a Rebel*.

25   Brutus, *Dennis Brutus Tapes*, 2.

26   Brutus, *Dennis Brutus Tapes*, 7.

27   Brutus, *Dennis Brutus Tapes*, 159.

28   Moloi, *I Am a Rebel*.

29   Moloi, *I Am a Rebel*.

30   Lewis, "Case for Asylum." *New York Times*, August 25, 1983.

31   Lewis, "Case for Asylum." *New York Times*, August 25, 1983.

32   Clendinen, "Black Poet, an Exile for 10 Years, Battles U.S. Deportation to Africa." *New York Times*, January 14, 1982.

33   Akindes and Dobo, "Homage to Dennis Brutus."

34   Egudu, *Modern African Poetry and the African Predicament*, 52.

35   Brutus, *Dennis Brutus Tapes*, 149.

36   Heywood, *South African Literature*, 142.

37   Brutus, *Dennis Brutus Tapes*, 172.

38   Brutus, "A Simple Lust."

39   Brutus, *Dennis Brutus Tapes*, 153.

40   http://www.sentinelpoetry.org.uk/slq/3.2/essays/olu-oguibe.htm.

41   *Democracy Now!*, 2009, 45:03.

42   "Dennis Brutus, Former Political Prisoner."

43   "Dennis Brutus, Former Political Prisoner."

44   "Copenhagen Dennis Brutus on Climate Change."

ENDNOTES

45   *Democracy Now!*, 2009, 51:45.

46   *Democracy Now!*, 2009, 52:54.

47   "Dennis Brutus (1924–2009): 'Political organiser and one of Africa's most celebrated poets.'"

48   Moloi, *I Am a Rebel.*

49   Email from Tony Brutus to author, March 18, 2020.

50   Luckie and Colbert, *Critical Perspectives on Dennis Brutus,* 206.

51   *Testimonials about Dennis Brutus,* 35.

52   *Testimonials about Dennis Brutus,* 3.

53   Moloi, *I Am a Rebel.*

54   Duodu, "Dennis Brutus obituary."

55   Akindes and Dobo, "Homage to Dennis Brutus."

56   Joseph, "Dennis Brutus."

57   Moloi, *I Am a Rebel.*

58   Moloi, *I Am a Rebel.*

Bibliography

Books and Articles

Brutus, Dennis. *The Dennis Brutus Tapes: Essays at Autobiography.* Edited by Bernth Lindfors. Woodbridge, UK: James Currey Publishing, 2011.

Brutus, Dennis. *Letters to Martha and Other Poems from a South African Prison.* Heinemann Educational, 1968.

Clendinen, Dudley. "Black Poet, an Exile for 10 Years, Battles U.S. Deportation to Africa." *The New York Times*, January 14, 1982.

Crompton, Samuel Willard. *Nelson Mandela: Ending Apartheid in South Africa.* New York: Chelsea House Publishers, 2007.

Egudu, R. N., *Modern African Poetry and the African Predicament*, Macmillan Press, 1978.

Espy, Richard. *The Politics of the Olympic Games.* Berkeley: University of California Press, 1979.

Heywood, Christopher, ed. *Aspects of South African Literature.* London: Heinemann Educational Books, 1976.

Lewis, Anthony. "Case for Asylum." *New York Times*, August 26, 1983.

BIBLIOGRAPHY

Luckie, Craig W. and Patrick J. Colbert, eds. *Critical Perspectives on Dennis Brutus*. Lynne Rienner Publishers, 1995.

Mandela, Nelson. *Conversations with Myself.* New York: Farrar, Straus and Giroux, 2010.

Videos

Moloi, Vincent, dir. *Dennis Brutus: I Am a Rebel*. Produced by Ben Cashdan and Vincent Moloi. Video, 53:45. Posted to YouTube May 27, 2013. www.youtube.com/watch?v=lNAfhW_kzn0&feature =youtu.be.

Field, Connie, dir. "Nelson Mandela: Dennis Brutus Helps Hide Mandela.*" In Have You Heard from Johannesburg: Seven Stories of the Global Anti-Apartheid Movement*. Clarity Films, 2010. Video, 1:37. Clip posted to YouTube December 16, 2013. www.youtube.com /watch?v=bToRXOZmHns&feature=youtu.be.

Akindes, Gerard, and Ken Dobo, producers. "Homage to Dennis Brutus: 1924–2009." Featuring Zakes Mda. Sports in Africa: Politics and Globalization, March 5–6, 2010. Ohio University. Video, 10:09. Posted to YouTube June 28, 2010. www.youtube.com/watch?v= c7j7uEWMu5k&feature=youtu.be.

Brutus, Dennis. "A Simple Lust." Video recording of Dennis Brutus reading his poem. Recorded by Graham Stewart at the Centre for the Study of Southern African Literature and Languages (CSSALL), University of Durban-Westville (UDW), Durban, South Africa. September 26, 1997. Video, 3:35. Posted to YouTube March 2, 2010. www.youtube.com/watch?v=NeHS9Ed_9Hc&feature=youtu.be.

"Dennis Brutus (1924–2009): South African Poet and Activist Dies in

Cape Town." Video airing including clips of Dennis Brutus interview from 2005. December 28, 2009. Video, 59:05. https://www.democracy now.org/2009/12/28/dennis_brutus_1924_2009_south_african.

"Dennis Brutus, Former Political Prisoner from South Africa." Video recording of Dennis Brutus speaking at SweatFree Communities conference in Philadelphia. July 12, 2008. Video, 3:52. Posted to YouTube July 19, 2008. www.youtube.com /watch?v=bjPO78v17Gc&feature=youtu.be.

"Copenhagen Dennis Brutus on Climate Change." YouTube video. Posted by "keithsam1," December 9, 2009. https://www.youtube. com/watch?v=pIxNNjV4y7g&feature=emb_logo

From the Web
South African History Online: Towards a People's History (website). "South Africa and the Olympic Games." Accessed May 30, 2020. www.sahistory.org.za/article/south-africa-and-olympic-games.

South African History Online: Towards a People's History (web- site). "Dennis Brutus." Accessed May 30, 2020. www.sahistory.org. za/people/dennis-brutus.

"Dennis Brutus (1924–2009): 'Political organiser and one of Africa's most celebrated poets.'" *Europe Solidaire Sans Frontières*. December 26, 2009. http://europe-solidaire.org/spip.php?article16324.

"Dennis Brutus, Apartheid's Poetic Rebel." *The National* (United Arab Emirates). January 9, 2010. www.thenational.ae/uae /dennis-brutus-apartheid-s-poetic-rebel-1.494451.

Centre for Civil Society (website). "Dennis Brutus Online Archive." Accessed May 30, 2020. http://ccs.ukzn.ac.za/default.asp?4,79.

BIBLIOGRAPHY

Duodu, Cameron. "Dennis Brutus obituary." *The Guardian*, February 23, 2010.

Testimonials about Dennis Brutus: Excerpts from Institutions, Individuals and Media. Centre for Civil Society. Haymarket Books. Chicago, IL. Accessed May 30, 2020. http://ccs.ukzn.ac.za/files/Brutus%20Ebook%20layout-web.pdf.

Robinson, Jackie, and K. C. Jones. "Statement by Jackie Robinson and K. C. Jones on Behalf of American Athletes Protesting South Africa's Readmission to the 1968 Olympic Games." American Committee on Africa. February 8, 1968. http://kora.matrix.msu.edu/files/50/304/32-130-FEB-84-GMH%20ACOA%2068OlyState.pdf.

Joseph, Isaac. "Dennis Brutus—The Anti-Apartheid Activist, an Eclectic Poet." Africa 360 Degrees. August 6, 2019.

About the Author

CRAIG ELLENPORT is an author who resides in Massapequa, New York. He has written many nonfiction books for children and young adults. Ellenport earned a degree in journalism from Northwestern University, where he also received a Certificate in African Studies. As part of the African Studies curriculum, he took the African Literature course that was taught by Dennis Brutus.